For all portable keyboards *by Kenn*

THE COMPL
KEYBOARD PLAYER

BOOK 2

Amsco Publications
New York/London/Sydney/Cologne

Exclusive Distributors:
Music Sales Corporation
24 East 22nd Street,
New York, NY 10010 USA

Order No. AM 38316
International Standard Book Number: 0.8256.2446.0

Printed in the United States of America by
Vicks Lithograph and Printing Corporation

ABOUT THIS BOOK

In Book Two of The Complete Keyboard Player you take a giant step forward in reading musical notation.

Side by side with the single-finger chords, you continue your study of "fingered" chords, by far the most rewarding aspect of left hand accompaniment playing.

As the book progresses you play more and more fill-ins, double notes, and chords with your right hand, which helps give you that "professional" sound.

Although Book Two (like Book One of the series) is designed basically as a "teach yourself" method, teachers everywhere will find it ideal for training tomorrow's electronic keyboard players.

SHARPS, FLATS, AND NATURALS

1

This sign is a sharp: ♯

When you see a sharp written alongside a note, play the nearest available key (black or white) to the RIGHT of that note:—

written:

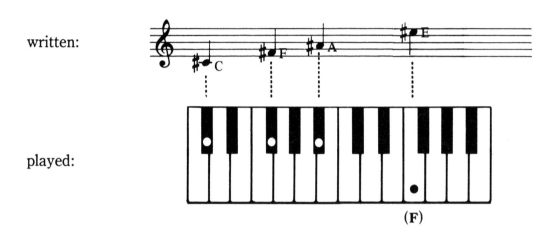

played:

(F)

Note: E sharp is simply an alternative way of writing "F".

This sign is a flat: ♭

When you see a flat written alongside a note, play the nearest available key (black or white) to the LEFT of that note:—

written:

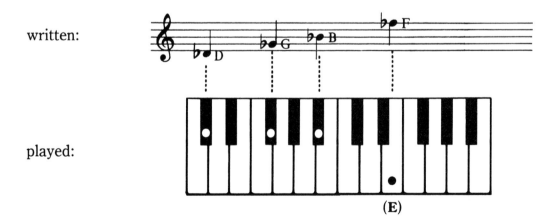

played:

(E)

Note: F flat is simply an alternative way of writing "E".

When a sharp or flat is written it continues as a sharp or flat right through the bar:—

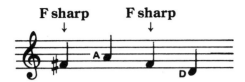

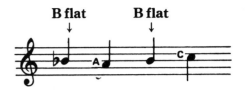

At the next bar, however, everything returns to normal:—

Apart from at the new bar, a sharp or flat may be cancelled any time by a sign called a "natural", ♮ :—

Look out for sharps, flats, and naturals in the pieces which follow.

GET BACK

Words & Music by John Lennon & Paul McCartney

Suggested registration: electric guitar
Rhythm: rock
Tempo: medium (♩ = 120)

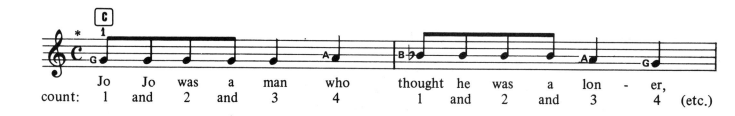

Jo Jo was a man who thought he was a lon - er,

count: 1 and 2 and 3 4   1 and 2 and 3 4 (etc.)

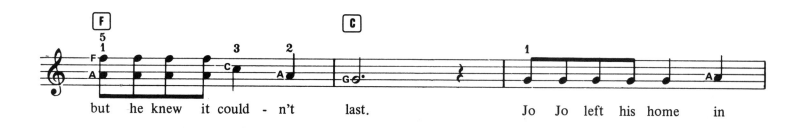

but he knew it could - n't last.   Jo Jo left his home in

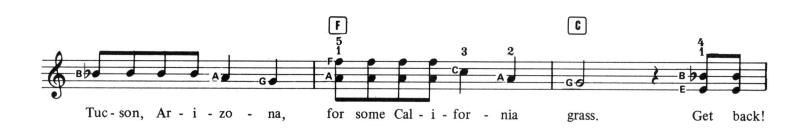

Tuc - son, Ar - i - zo - na,   for some Cal - i - for - nia   grass.   Get back!

Change finger on G

Get back!   Get back to where you once be -

longed .___   Get back!   Get back!   Get

---

* Common Time. An alternative way of writing **4/4**

back to where you once be - longed___ Sweet Lo - ret - ta Mod - ern

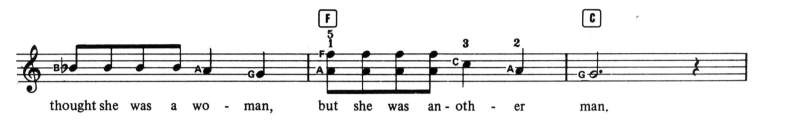

thought she was a wo - man, but she was an - oth - er man.

All the girls a - round her say she's got it com - ing, but she gets it while she

can. Get back! Get back! Get

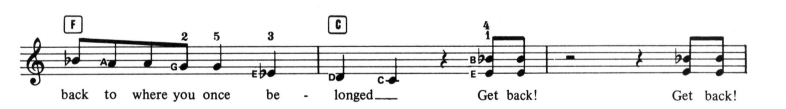

back to where you once be - longed___ Get back! Get back!

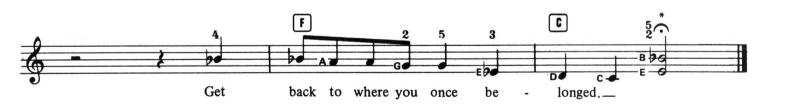

Get back to where you once be - longed.___

* **Pause (Fermata).** Hold the note(s) longer
than written (at the discretion of the performer).

PIGALLE

English Lyrics by Charles Newman
French Lyrics by Georges Ulmer & Geo Koger
Music by Georges Ulmer & Guy Luypaerts

Suggested registration: accordion +
chorus (chorale)

Rhythm: waltz
Tempo: fairly fast (♩ = 152)

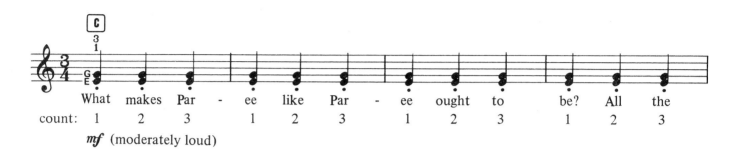

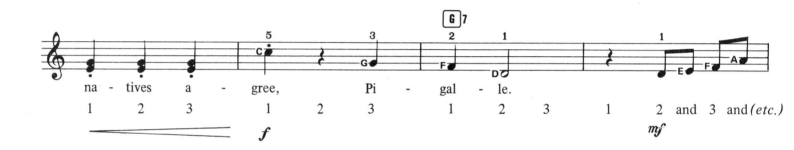

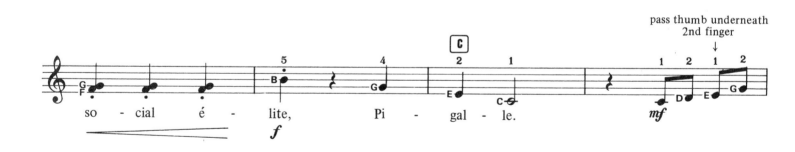

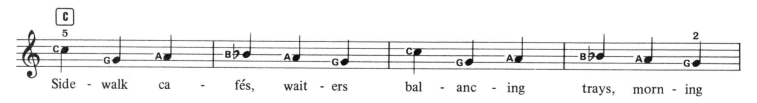

night, and noon. Tax - i cabs

toot, while a guy on a flute, fin - gers "Clair de

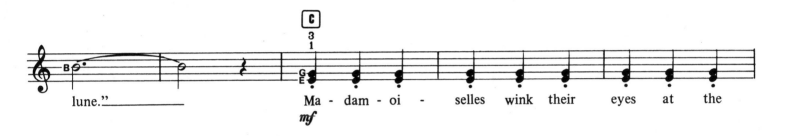

lune." Ma - dam - oi - selles wink their eyes at the

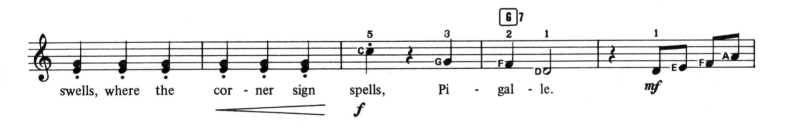

swells, where the cor - ner sign spells, Pi - gal - le.

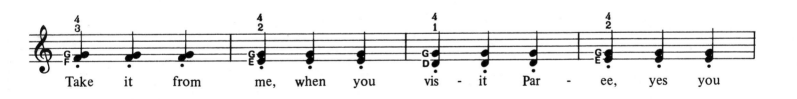

Take it from me, when you vis - it Par - ee, yes you

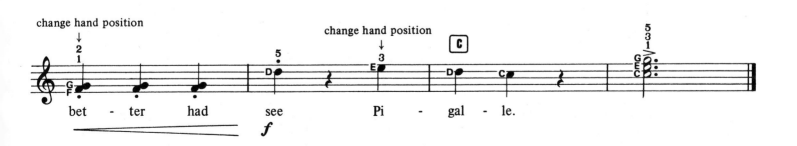

bet - ter had see Pi - gal - le.

ROCK AROUND THE CLOCK

Words & Music by Max C. Freedman & Jimmy
de Knight

Suggested registration: trumpet, or saxophone
Rhythm: swing
Tempo: fairly fast (♩ = 160)

Press rhythm start button (ordinary, not
synchro) with left hand, as right hand
strikes first note. Play through Verse
using melody and drums only. Start left
hand chords at Chorus.

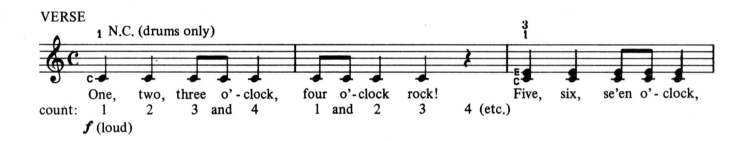

broad day - light, we're gon - na rock, gon - na rock a - round the clock to -

night._____ When the clock strikes two,

three and four, if the band slows down we'll yell for more, we're gon - na

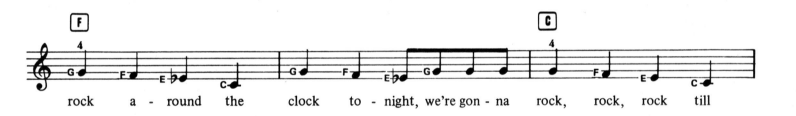

rock a - round the clock to - night, we're gon - na rock, rock, rock till

broad day - light, we're gon - na rock, gon - na rock a - round the clock to -

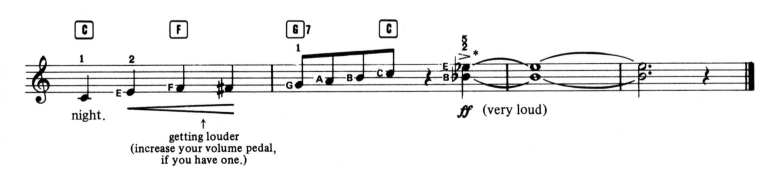

night. *ff* (very loud)

getting louder
(increase your volume pedal,
if you have one.)

* ACCENT

TWO NEW CHORDS: C7 AND A7

2

Using single-finger chord method:

Locate "C" and "A" in the accompaniment section of your keyboard. Convert these notes into "C7" and "A7" (see Book One, p. 42ff., and your owner's manual).

Using fingered chord method:

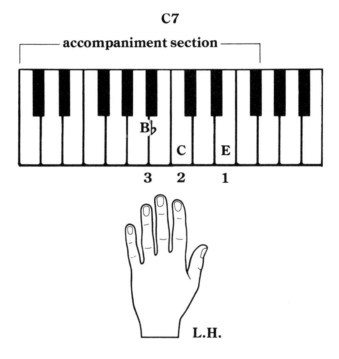

C7

L.H.

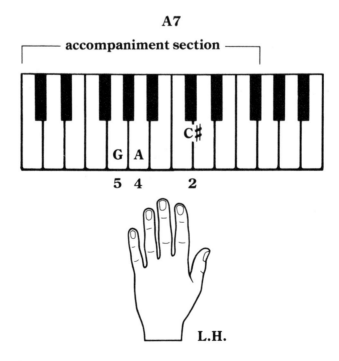

A7

L.H.

A NEW STAGE IN READING MUSIC

3 Up to now, in order to help you, letter names have appeared beside the written notes. These letters will now be discontinued.

Here's how you can learn the names of the notes:

The **staff** consists of five lines:—

remember this sentence:
Every **G**ood **B**oy **D**eserves **F**ruit

and four spaces:—

remember this word: **F A C E**

Learn the notes on the five lines, and the notes in the four spaces first. Then learn the "in-between" notes, like this:

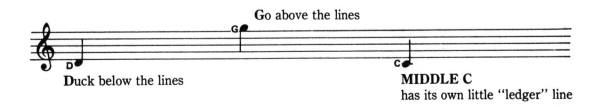

LET HIM GO, LET HIM TARRY

Traditional

Suggested registration: flute

Rhythm: bossa nova
Tempo: medium (♩ = 108)
Synchro-start, if available

Let him go, let him tar - ry, let him sink or let him

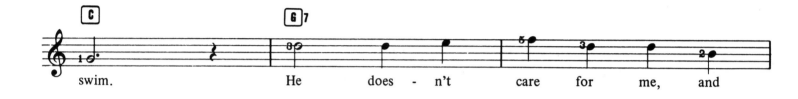

swim. He does - n't care for me, and

I don't care for him. He can go and get an -

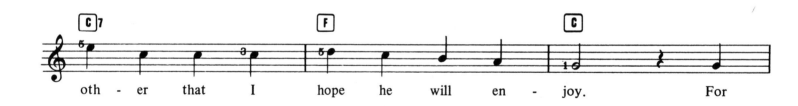

oth - er that I hope he will en - joy. For

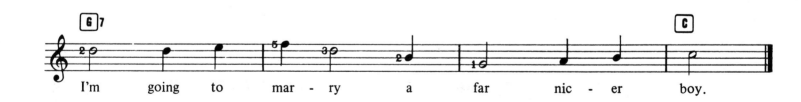

I'm going to mar - ry a far nic - er boy.

LOVE ME TENDER

Words & Music by Elvis Presley & Vera Matson

Suggested registration: string ensemble.
    Arpeggio optional.

Rhythm: rock
Tempo: medium (♩ = 96)

Love me ten - der, love me sweet, nev - er let me

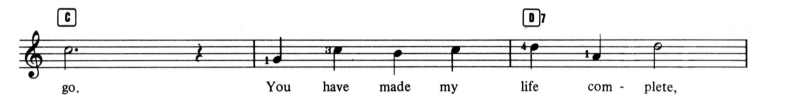

go. You have made my life com - plete,

and I love you so. Love me ten - der,

love me true, all my dreams ful - fil.

For, my dar - lin', I love you, and I al - ways will.

DAL SEGNO AL CODA (D.S. AL CODA)

4 A **Coda** is a section, usually quite short, added to a piece of music to make an ending.

Dal Segno al Coda (D.S. al Coda) means go back to the sign: 𝄋 and play through the same music again, until:

to coda ⊕

From here jump to CODA and play through to the end.

SOMETHIN' STUPID

Words & Music by C. Carson Parks

Suggested registration: accordion

Rhythm: cha-cha (or rhumba)
Tempo: medium (♩ = 112)
Synchro-start, if available

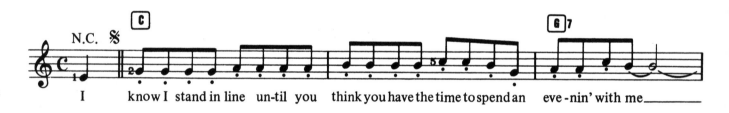

I know I stand in line un-til you think you have the time to spend an eve-nin' with me_____

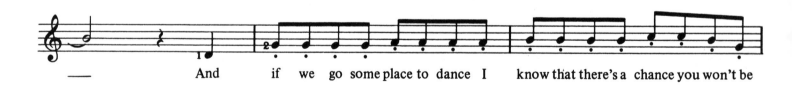

___ And if we go some place to dance I know that there's a chance you won't be

leav-in' with me._____ Then af-ter-wards we drop in-to a

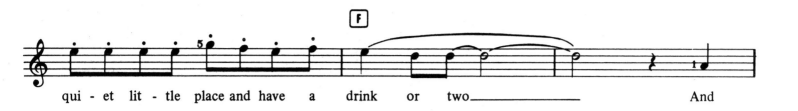

qui - et lit - tle place and have a drink or two_____ And

then I go and spoil it all by say - in' some-thin' stu-pid like "I love you."_____

Change accordion
to clarinet

_____ I can see it in your eyes that you de - spise the same old lies you heard the

night be - fore_____ And though it's just a line to you, for

clarinet to accordion
D.%. al Coda

me it's true and nev - er seemed so right be - fore._____ I

love you."

ARE YOU LONESOME TONIGHT

Words & Music by Roy Turk & Lou Handman

Suggested registration: flute + full sustain

Rhythm: waltz
Tempo: fairly slow (♩ = 80)
Synchro-start, if available

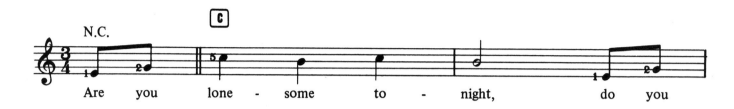

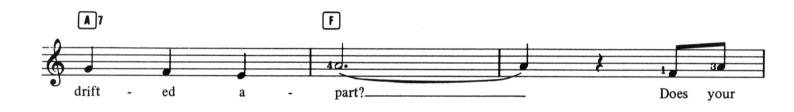

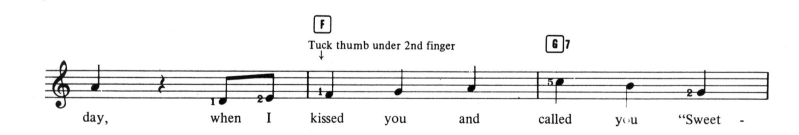

heart?" Do the chairs in your

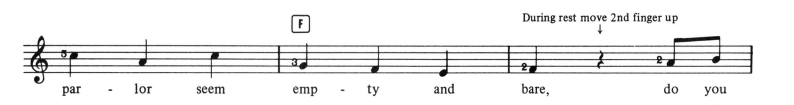

par - lor seem emp - ty and bare, do you

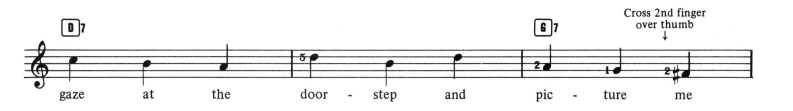

gaze at the door - step and pic - ture me there?

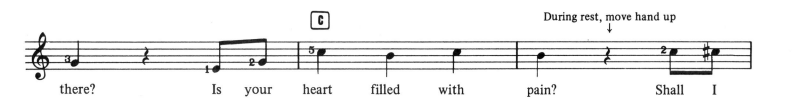

there? Is your heart filled with pain? Shall I

come back a - gain? Tell me dear, are you

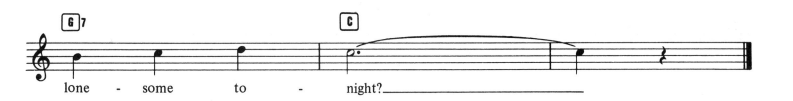

lone - some to - night?

AN APPLE FOR THE TEACHER

Words by Johnny Burke
Music by James V. Monaco

Suggested registration: trombone, or horn

Rhythm: swing
Tempo: fairly fast (♩ = 176)
Synchro-start, if available

An ap - ple for the teach - er, that

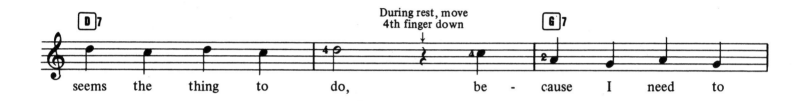

seems the thing to do, be - cause I need to

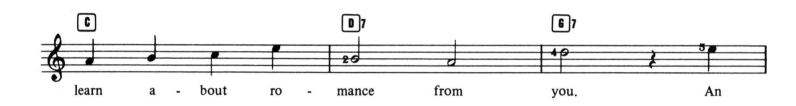

learn a - bout ro - mance from you. An

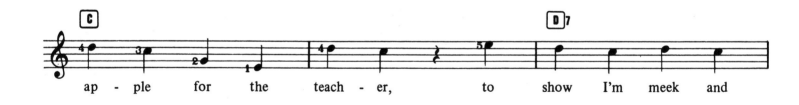

ap - ple for the teach - er, to show I'm meek and

mild. If you in - sist on say - ing that I'm

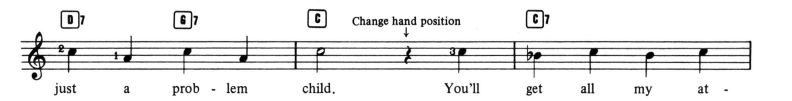

just a prob-lem child. You'll get all my at -

ten - tion, your wish will be my rule; and

may - be you'll be good to me and keep me af - ter

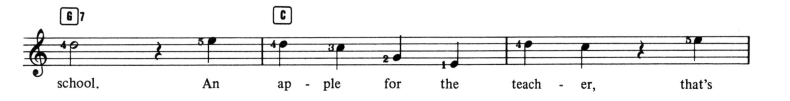

school. An ap - ple for the teach - er, that's

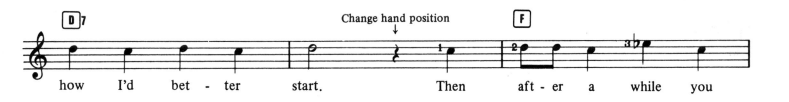

how I'd bet - ter start. Then aft - er a while you

may give in and let me bring my heart.

THREE NEW NOTES FOR RIGHT HAND: LOW G, A, B

These three notes lie directly to the left of Middle C. The lowest of them, G, probably forms the left hand extremity of the "melody section" on your instrument.

I have placed letter names beside the new notes only in the next few songs.

GUANTANAMERA

Words by Jose Marti
Music adaptation by Hector Angulo & Pete Seeger

Suggested registration: flute, + duet (if available)

Rhythm: bossa nova
Tempo: medium (♩ = 100)

cre - ce la pal - ma.___ Yo soy un hom - bre sin - ce - ro___

De don - de cre - ce la pal - ma___ Y an - tes de

mo - rir - me quie - ro, E - char mis ver - sos del al -

ma. Guan - ta - na - me - ra___ gua - ji - ra

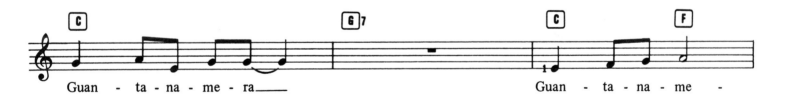

Guan - ta - na - me - ra___ Guan - ta - na - me -

ra, gua - ji - ra Guan - ta - na - me - ra!

BILL BAILEY WON'T YOU PLEASE COME HOME

Traditional

Suggested registration: piano, or honky-tonk
piano

Rhythm: swing
Tempo: fairly fast (♩ = 176)

"Won't   you   come   home,   Bill   Bai - ley?

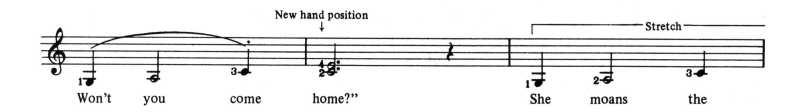

Won't   you   come   home?"   She   moans   the

whole   day   long._____

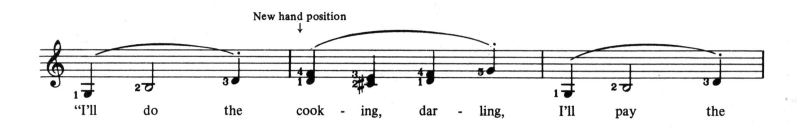

"I'll   do   the   cook - ing,   dar - ling,   I'll   pay   the

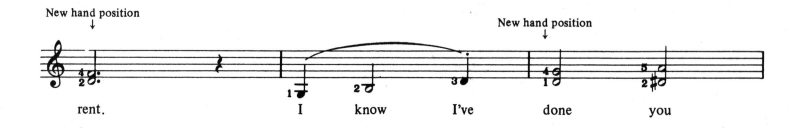

rent.   I   know   I've   done   you

wrong _____ 'Mem - ber that

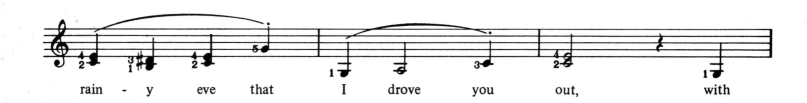

rain - y eve that I drove you out, with

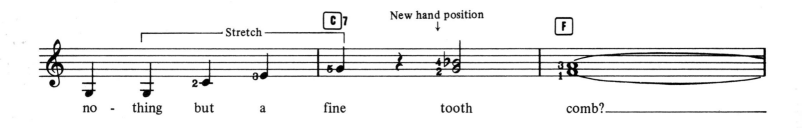

no - thing but a fine tooth comb? _____

_____ I know I'm to blame, well,

ain't that a shame? Bill Bai - ley won't you

please come home?" Stop rhythm

DA CAPO AL CODA (D.C. AL CODA)

6 **Da Capo** means "from the beginning".

Da Capo al Coda (D.C. al Coda) means go back to the beginning of the piece and play through the same music

again, until: to coda ⊕

From here jump to CODA and play through to the end.

THIS NEARLY WAS MINE

Words by Oscar Hammerstein II
Music by Richard Rodgers

Suggested registration: string ensemble

Rhythm: waltz
Tempo: slow (♩ = 80)

MINOR CHORDS

7 The MINOR CHORD is another important type of chord.

When using the single-finger chord function, there are various ways of forming minor chords. Your owner's manual will tell you how to form minor chords on your particular instrument. The first two diagrams in 8, on the next page, show two possibilities.

CHORD OF F MINOR (Fm)

8 Using single-finger chord method:

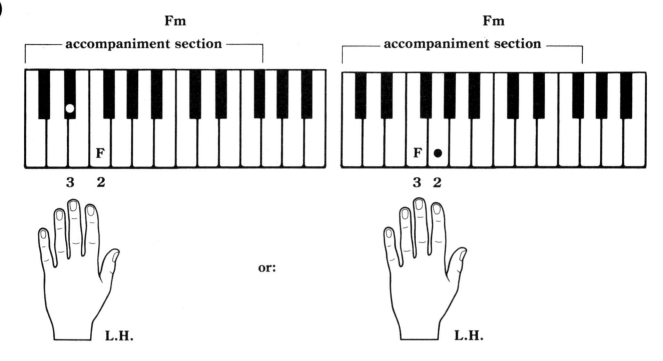

or:

play F, together with any black note to its **LEFT**.

play F, together with any (one) note to its **RIGHT**.

Using fingered chord method:

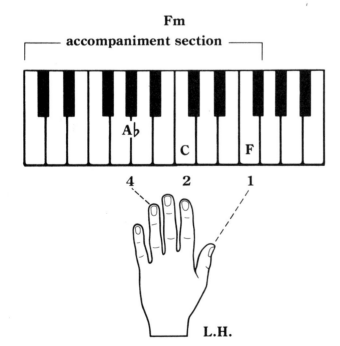

DOTTED TIME NOTES

9 A dot after a note adds half as much time again to that note:—

	lasting
♩ half note (minim)	2 beats
♩. dotted half note (dotted minim)	2 + 1 = 3 beats
♩ quarter note (crotchet)	1 beat
♩. dotted quarter note (dotted crotchet)	1 + ½ = 1½ beats

DOTTED QUARTER NOTE (DOTTED CROTCHET)

10 A Dotted Quarter Note, ♩., worth 1½ beats, usually combines with an Eighth Note (Quaver), ♪, worth ½ beat, to make two whole beats:—

♩. ♪	1½ + ½ = 2 beats
or: ♪ ♩.	½ + 1½ = 2 beats

The first of these two time note combinations: ♩. ♪ is the more common. This is how you count it:—

WHAT KIND OF FOOL AM I, p.30

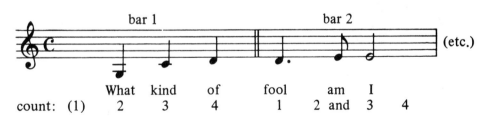

Notice how the "dot" delays note D, so that the next note (E) falls on an "and" beat. The situation is always the same with this rhythm.

Look out for other examples of dotted quarter note/quaver combinations in the songs which follow.

WHAT KIND OF FOOL AM I

(FROM THE MUSICAL PRODUCTION "STOP THE WORLD I WANT TO GET OFF")

Words & Music by Leslie Bricusse & Anthony Newley

Suggested registration: piano

Rhythm: bossa nova
Tempo: medium (♩ = 100)
Synchro-start, if available

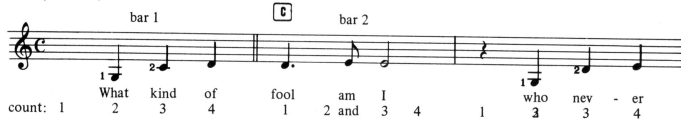

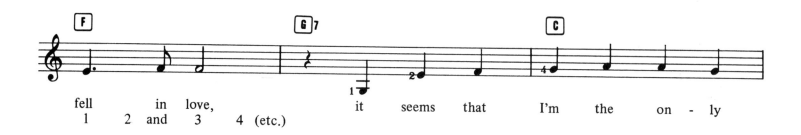

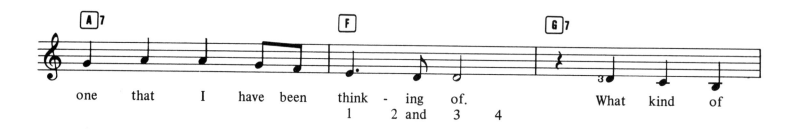

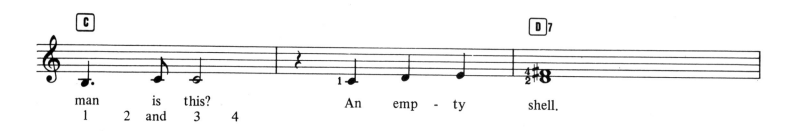

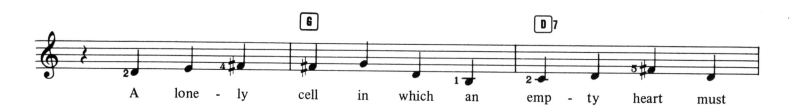

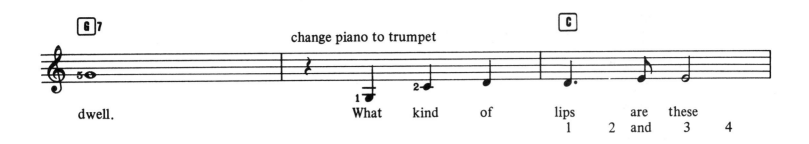

dwell.   change piano to trumpet   What kind of lips are these
                                                   1   2 and 3   4

that lied with ev - 'ry kiss?   That whis - pered
1   2 and 3   4

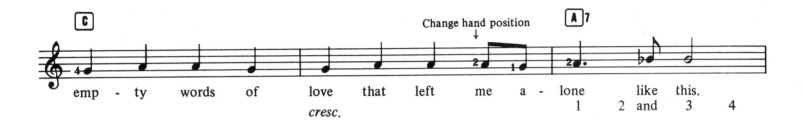

Change hand position

emp - ty words of love that left me a - lone like this.
cresc.   1   2 and 3   4

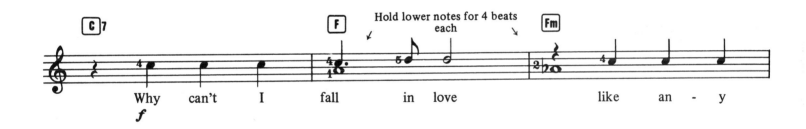

Hold lower notes for 4 beats
each

Why can't I fall in love   like an - y
f

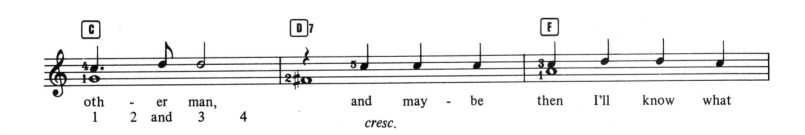

oth - er man,   and may - be then I'll know what
1   2 and 3   4   cresc.

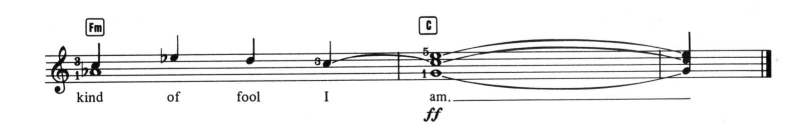

kind of fool I am. _____
ff

LOVE'S ROUNDABOUT
(LA RONDE DE L'AMOUR)

French Words by Louis Ducreux
English Words by Harold Purcell
Music by Oscar Straus

Suggested registration: accordion
+ arpeggio (if available)

Rhythm: waltz
Tempo: fairly fast (♩ = 160)

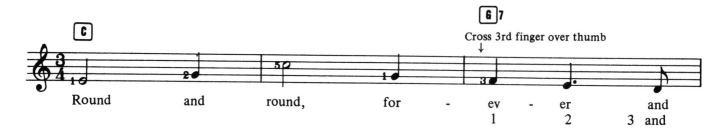

Cross 3rd finger over thumb

Round and round, for - ev - er and
1 2 3 and

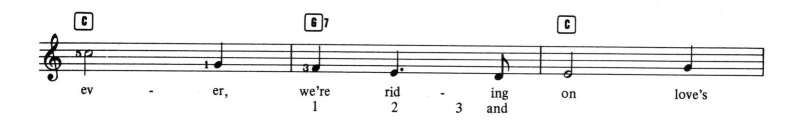

ev - er, we're rid - ing on love's
1 2 3 and

round - a - bout; rich or

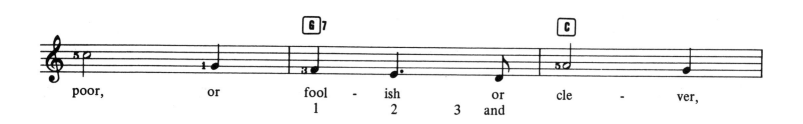

poor, or fool - ish or cle - ver,
1 2 3 and

round we must go, year in, year
1 2 3 and

Change accordion to clarinet

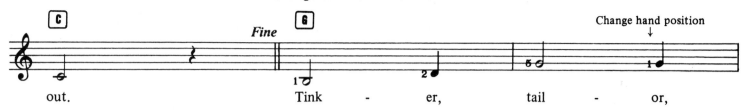

Change hand position

out.　　　　　　　　　　Tink　-　er,　　　tail　-　or,

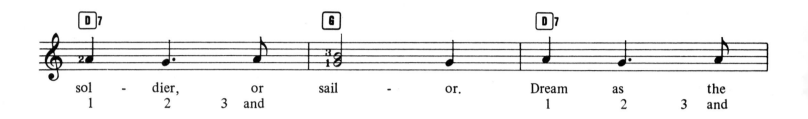

sol　-　dier,　　　or　　　sail　　-　　or.　　　Dream　　　as　　　the
1　　　　2　　　3　and　　　　　　　　　　1　　　2　　　3　and

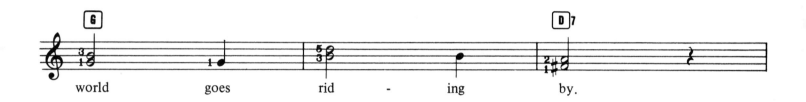

world　　　　goes　　　rid　-　ing　　　by.

Turn　　　the　　　pag　-　es　　　back　　thro'　　　the
　　　　　　　　　　　　　　　　　　　　　　1　　　2　　　3　and

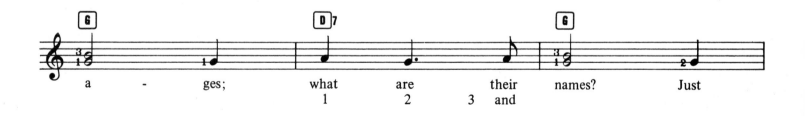

a　-　ges;　　　what　　are　　their　　names?　　　Just
　　　　　　　　1　　　2　　　3　and

Cross 2nd finger
over thumb
↓

Change clarinet to accordion
*D.C. al FINE

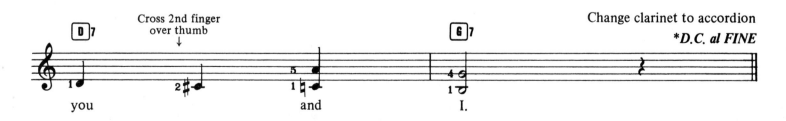

you　　　　　　　　and　　　　I.

* **Da Capo Al Fine.** Go back to the beginning
of the piece and play through the same music
again until FINE (the end).

STARDUST

Words by Mitchell Parish
Music by Hoagy Carmichael

Suggested registration: vibraphone, or celeste,
 + full sustain

Rhythm: swing
Tempo: fairly slow (♩ = 80)
Synchro-start, if available

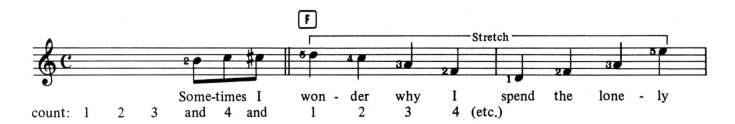

count: 1   2   3   and 4   and   1   2   3   4   (etc.)

Some-times I won-der why I spend the lone-ly

night   dream-ing of a song,   the mel - o - dy

haunts my re-ve-rie.   And I am once a-gain with you.   When our

love was new,   and each kiss an in-spi - ra - tion____

____   But that was long a - go, now my con-so-la-tion is

in the star-dust of a song. Be - side a gar-den

wall when stars are bright, you are in my arms. The

night - in - gale tells his fair - y tale of par - a -dise where ros - es

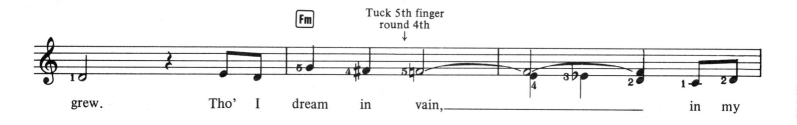

grew. Tho' I dream in vain, in my

heart it will re - main. My star - dust mel - o - dy,

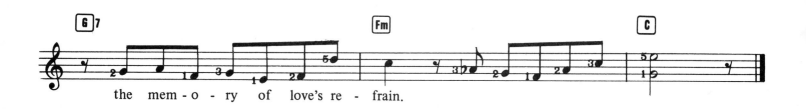

the mem - o - ry of love's re - frain.

CHORD OF D MINOR (Dm), AND CHORD OF A MINOR (Am)

11

Using single-finger chord method:

Locate D (the higher one), and A, in the accompaniment section of your keyboard. Convert these notes into "Dm" and

"Am" respectively (see Book two, P. 28, and your owner's manual).

Using fingered chord method:

Dm

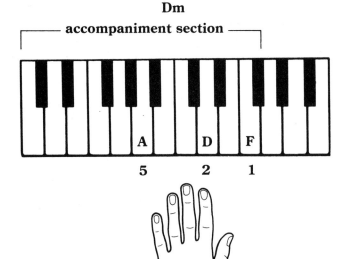

Am

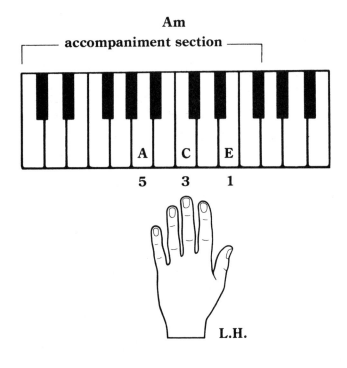

SCARBOROUGH FAIR

Traditional

Suggested registration: flute

Rhythm: waltz
Tempo: slow (♩ = 84)

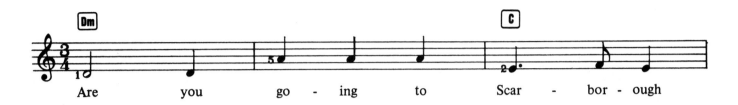

Are you go - ing to Scar - bor - ough

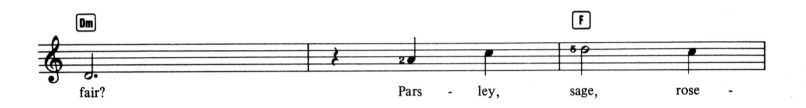

fair? Pars - ley, sage, rose -

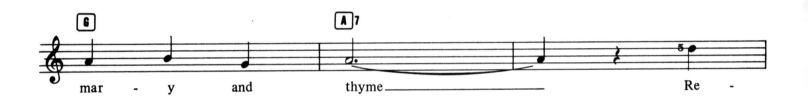

mar - y and thyme _____ Re -

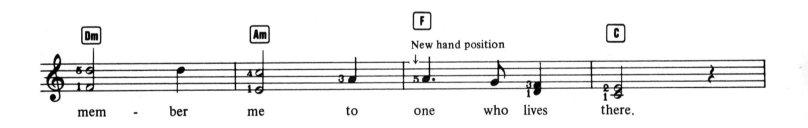

New hand position

mem - ber me to one who lives there.

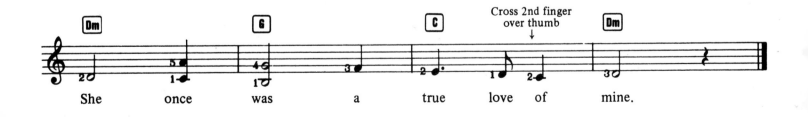

Cross 2nd finger
over thumb

She once was a true love of mine.

TAKE ME HOME, COUNTRY ROADS

Words & Music by Bill Danoff, Taffy Nivert &
John Denver

Suggested registration: piano, or electric piano
+ half sustain

Rhythm: swing
Tempo: quite fast (♩ = 192)

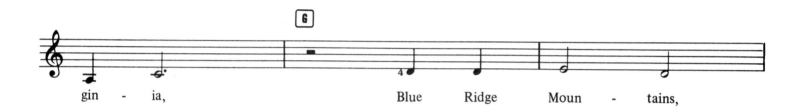

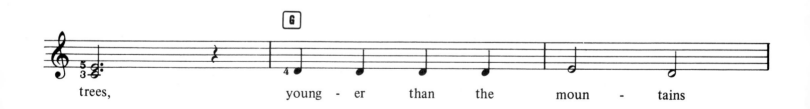

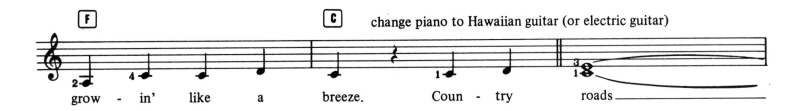

change piano to Hawaiian guitar (or electric guitar)

grow - in' like a breeze. Coun - try roads

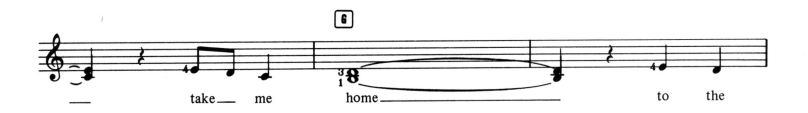

take me home to the

place I be - long:

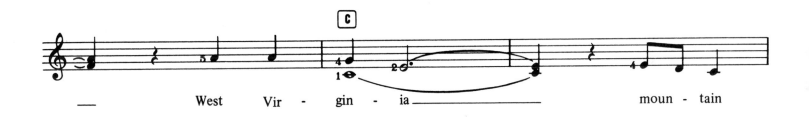

West Vir - gin - ia moun - tain

mom - ma, take me home

coun - try roads.

THREE NEW NOTES FOR RIGHT HAND:
HIGH A, B, C

12

If you have a 44, or a 49 note keyboard,
these will be your top three notes.

I have placed letter names beside the new
notes in the next few songs.

SAILING

Words & Music by Gavin Sutherland

Suggested registration: *jazz organ*
  + sustain

Rhythm: *disco*
Tempo: slow (♩ = 69); but run rhythm at double speed
(♩ = 138)
Synchro-start, if available

* Pause on each note, for dramatic effect.

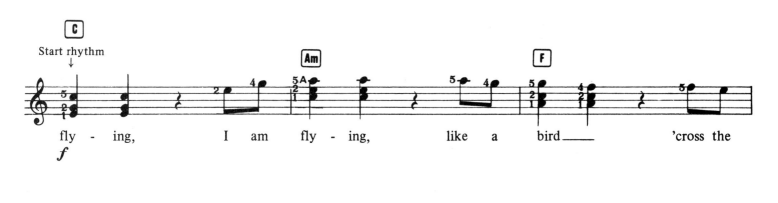

fly - ing, I am fly - ing, like a bird ___ 'cross the

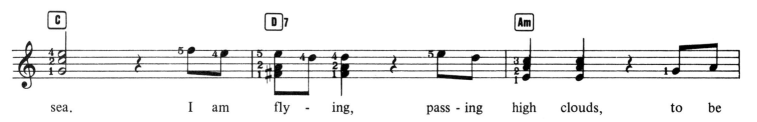

sea. I am fly - ing, pass - ing high clouds, to be

near ___ you, to be free. We are sail - ing, we are

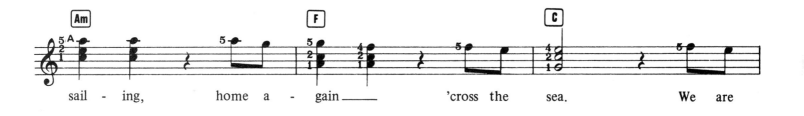

sail - ing, home a - gain ___ 'cross the sea. We are

sail - ing storm - y wa - ters, to be near ___ you, to be

free. To be near ___ you, to be free.

I CAN'T GIVE YOU ANYTHING BUT LOVE

Words by Dorothy Fields
Music by Jimmy McHugh

Suggested registration: piano

Rhythm: swing
Tempo: medium (♩ = 120)

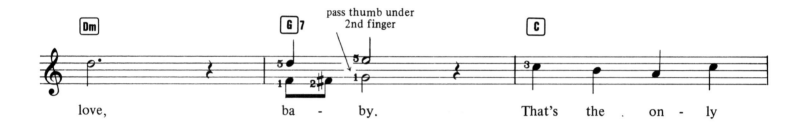

I can't give you an - y - thing but love,

ba - by. That's the on - ly

thing I've plen - ty of, ba - by.

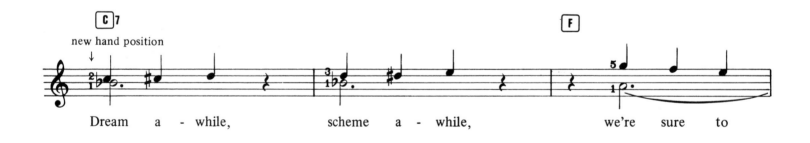

new hand position

Dream a - while, scheme a - while, we're sure to

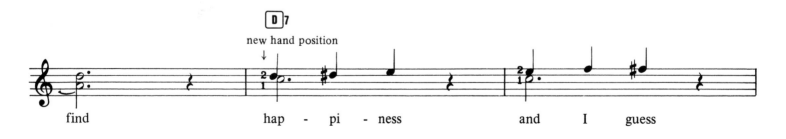

new hand position

find hap - pi - ness and I guess

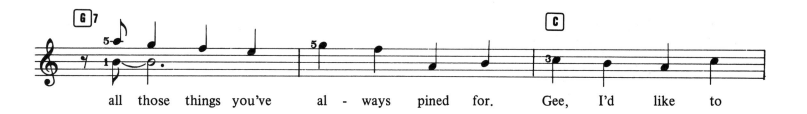

all those things you've al - ways pined for. Gee, I'd like to

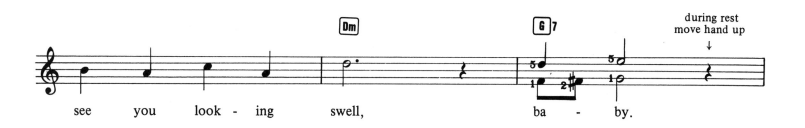

see you look - ing swell, ba - by.

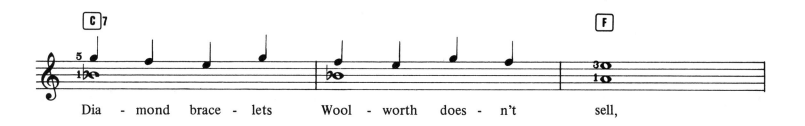

Dia - mond brace - lets Wool - worth does - n't sell,

ba - by. Till that luck - y day you know darned

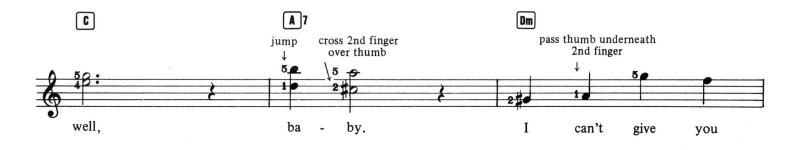

well, ba - by. I can't give you

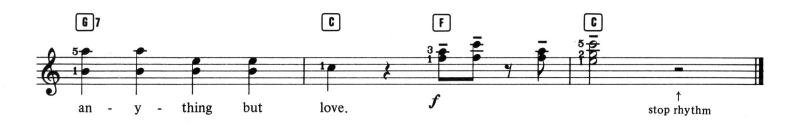

an - y - thing but love.

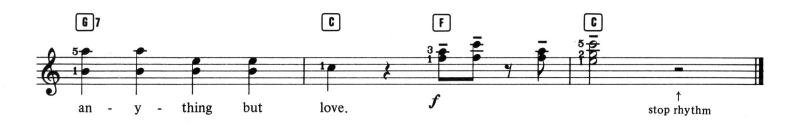

CRUISING DOWN THE RIVER

Words & Music by Eily Beadell & Nell Tollerton

Suggested registration: accordion

Rhythm: waltz
Tempo: fairly fast (♩ = 152)

Cruis - ing down the ri - ver

on a Sun - day af - ter -

noon. With one you

Cross 3rd finger over 4th

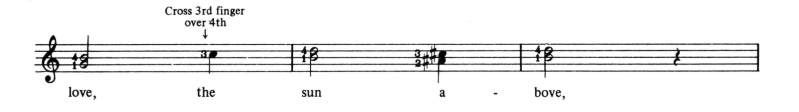

love, the sun a - bove,

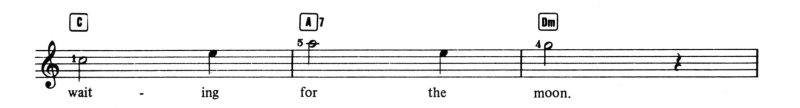

wait - ing for the moon.

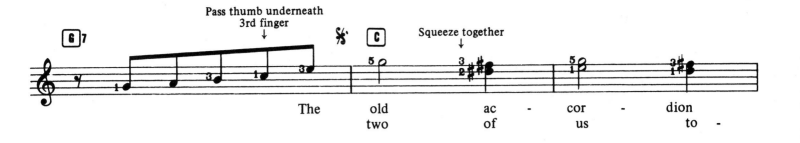

Pass thumb underneath
3rd finger

G7   C   Squeeze together

The old ac - cor - dion
two of us to -

A7   Move hand down   D7

play - ing_____ a sen - ti a -
geth - er_____ we'll plan a

men - tal tune.
hon - ey - moon.

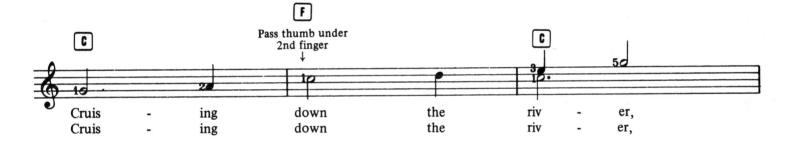

F   Pass thumb under
2nd finger

C   C

Cruis - ing down the riv - er,
Cruis - ing down the riv - er,

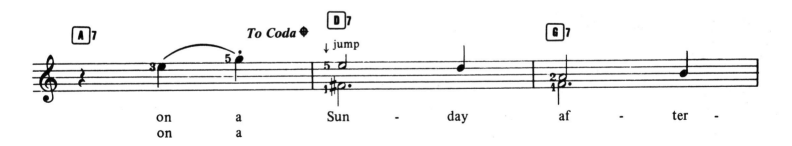

A7   To Coda ✦   D7   ↓ jump   G7

on a Sun - day af - ter -
on a

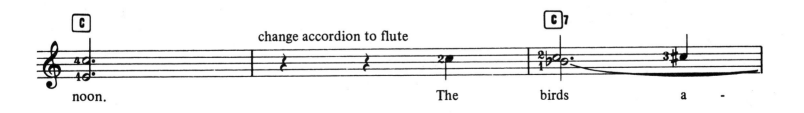

C   change accordion to flute   C7

noon.   The birds a -

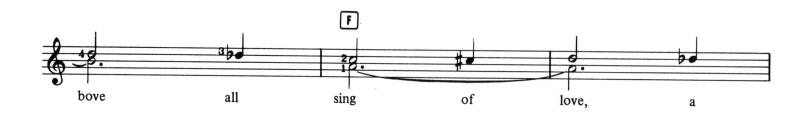

bove all sing of love, a

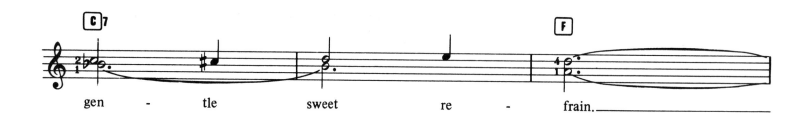

gen - tle sweet re - frain._____

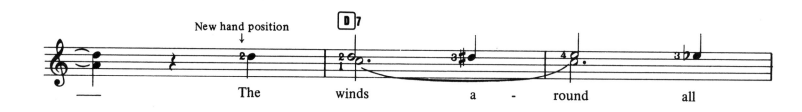

The winds a - round all

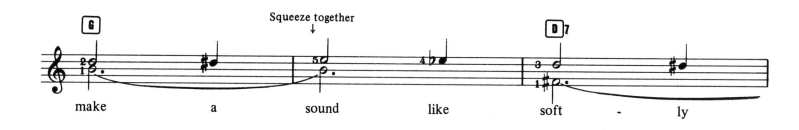

make a sound like soft - ly

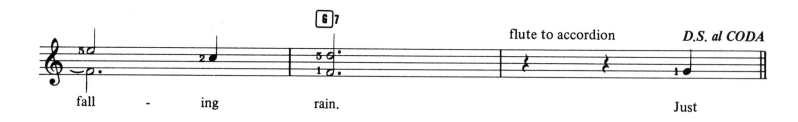

fall - ing rain. Just

Sun - day af - ter - noon.

cresc.　　　　　　*f*　　　　Stop rhythm

46

HELLO GOODBYE

Words & Music by John Lennon & Paul McCartney

Suggested registration: electric guitar

Rhythm: rock
Tempo: medium (♩ = 112)

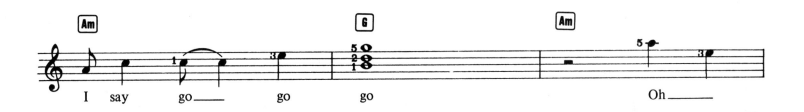

You say yes___ I say no___ you say stop___ and

I say go___ go go Oh___

no. You say good - bye, and I say hel -

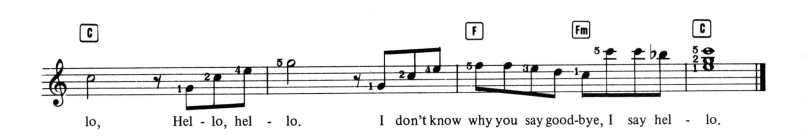

lo, Hel - lo, hel - lo. I don't know why you say good-bye, I say hel -

lo, Hel - lo, hel - lo. I don't know why you say good-bye, I say hel - lo.

LAST WORD

13 Congratulations on reaching the end of Book Two of The Complete Keyboard Player.

In Book Three you will

- improve your note reading

- learn new chords

- play in new keys, including "minor" keys

- develop further your sense of rhythm

- add those important professional touches to your playing.

CHORD CHART (Showing all "fingered chords" used in the course so far)

14

C

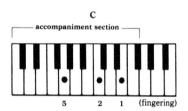

C7

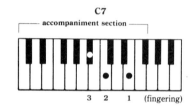

G

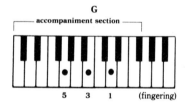

G7

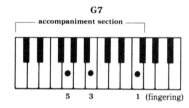

F

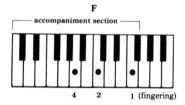

Fm

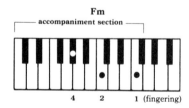

Dm

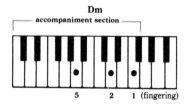

D7

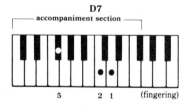

Am

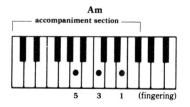

A7

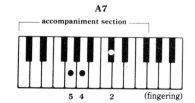